BOMBAY CATS

abdopublishing.com

Published by Abdo Publishing, a division of ABDO, PO Box 398166, Minneapolis, Minnesota 55439.

Big Buddy Books™ is a trademark and logo of Abdo Publishing.

Printed in the United States of America, North Mankato, Minnesota.
092017
012018

Cover Photo: Getty Images.
Interior Photos: Andrey Kuzmichev/Shutterstock (p. 15); Cedric Girard/Biosphoto/ardea.com (p. 25); cynoclub/depositphotos (p. 27); dionoanomalia/depositphotos (p. 5); Getty Images (pp. 7, 9, 11, 19, 25); Jaroslaw Kurek (p. 13); Jarred Moore (p. 17); serkucher (p. 29); Shutterstock (pp. 21, 23).

Coordinating Series Editor: Tamara L. Britton
Contributing Editor: Jill Roesler
Graphic Design: Jenny Christensen

Publisher's Cataloging-in-Publication Data

Names: Lajiness, Katie, author.
Title: Bombay cats / by Katie Lajiness.
Description: Minneapolis, Minnesota : Abdo Publishing, 2018. | Series: Big buddy cats | Includes online resources and index.
Identifiers: LCCN 2017943920 | ISBN 9781532111969 (lib.bdg.) | ISBN 9781614799030 (ebook)
Subjects: LCSH: Bombay cat--Juvenile literature. | Cats--Juvenile literature.
Classification: DDC 636.822--dc23
LC record available at https://lccn.loc.gov/2017943920

CONTENTS

A POPULAR BREED

Cats are popular pets. About 35 percent of US households have a cat. And, Americans own more than 85 million!

Around the world, there are more than 40 **domestic cat breeds**. One of these is the Bombay cat. Let's learn why the Bombay is a popular cat breed in the United States.

Today, there are about 600 million domestic cats in the world!

THE CAT FAMILY

All cats belong to the **Felidae** family. There are 37 **species** in this family. **Domestic cats** are part of one species. Lions and other types of cats make up the others.

Did you know?

Humans and cats have lived together for at least 3,500 years.

US families have more pet cats than any other country.

BOMBAY CATS

In 1953, **breeder** Nikki Horner **bred** a Burmese cat with a black American shorthair. Horner named the kittens Bombays because they looked like small black panthers.

Did you know?

Black leopards live in Asia and Africa. Black jaguars live in South America. But all big cats with black fur are sometimes called black panthers.

The Bombay breed is a cross between a black American shorthair (*left*) and a Burmese (*right*).

From 1966 to 1972, Horner **bred** 27 **litters**. Throughout the early 1970s, she worked to create a Bombay breed club.

Over time, Horner added at least 100 Bombay cats to the **registry**. The Bombay was fully recognized in 1978 by the **Cat Fanciers' Association**. It even received a **championship** status!

Cats can hear better than dogs or humans.

WHAT THEY'RE LIKE

The Bombay is a very loving **breed**. They are lively cats that jump on laps and beg for attention. As loyal pets, these cats love their owners and follow them around.

Did you know?

A group of cats is called a clowder.

The Bombay name comes from the cat's similarities to an Indian leopard.

COAT AND COLOR

Bombay cats have short, glossy black coats. Their fur is always solid black. Even the pads on the bottom of their paws are black!

All kittens are born with blue eyes. At about one year old, a Bombay's eyes turn copper or gold.

SIZE

This **breed** is muscular and compact. A Bombay's head, eyes, chin, and paws are round.

Adult males weigh eight to 11 pounds (4 to 5 kg). Females weigh somewhat less.

Bombay cats can play fetch! They are also good at walking on a leash.

FEEDING

Healthy cat food includes beef, chicken, or fish. A good name-brand food will provide the **nutrients** a cat needs.

Cat food can be dry, semimoist, or canned. Food labels will show how much and how often to feed a cat.

Every day, cats need
food and fresh water.

CARE

The Bombay requires little **grooming** because this **breed** does not shed much. A cat should have its claws trimmed every ten to 14 days. It should also have its ears checked to avoid **infection**.

When preparing for a cat show, bathe a Bombay three days before. This way, its coat can regain its natural shine.

Bombay cats need a good veterinarian. The vet can provide health exams and **vaccines**. He or she can also **spay** or **neuter** cats.

Kittens need to see the vet several times during their first few months. Adult cats should visit the vet once a year for a checkup.

About 90 percent of pet cats in the United States are spayed or neutered.

Cats have an **instinct** to bury their waste. So, cats should use a **litter box**. Waste should be removed from the box daily.

A cat buries its waste to mark its area. If a cat goes outdoors, it will begin to do the same. A **microchip** can help bring a cat home if it gets lost.

Did you know?

A scratching post provides a spot for a cat to sharpen its claws. That way, the cat won't scratch the furniture.

Domestic cats enjoy the outdoors. But they will live longer if kept inside.

KITTENS

A Bombay mother is **pregnant** for 63 to 65 days. Then, she gives birth to a **litter** of about six kittens. For the first two weeks, kittens mostly eat and sleep.

All kittens are born blind and deaf. After two weeks, they can see and hear. At three weeks, the kittens begin taking their first steps.

In seven years, a cat family could produce up to 420,000 kittens!

THINGS THEY NEED

Between 12 and 16 weeks old, Bombay kittens are ready for **adoption**. Kittens like to be active. So, they need daily exercise. A Bombay will be a loving companion for about 16 years.

Bombays are smart cats that love to play. They need a lot of attention from their owners.

GLOSSARY

adoption the process of taking responsibility for a pet.

breed a group of animals sharing the same appearance and features. To breed is to produce animals by mating.

breeder someone who breeds animals.

Cat Fanciers' Association established in 1906, it is the world's largest registry for pedigreed cats.

championship an event held to find a first-place winner.

domestic cats tame cats that make great pets.

Felidae the scientific Latin name for the cat family. Members of this family are called felines. They include domestic cats, lions, tigers, lynx, and cheetahs.

groom to clean and care for.

infection (Ihn-FEHK-shuhn) the causing of an unhealthy condition by something harmful, such as bacteria.

instinct a way of behaving, thinking, or feeling that is not learned, but natural.

litter all of the kittens born at one time to a mother cat.

litter box a place for house cats to leave their waste.

microchip an electronic circuit placed under an animal's skin. A microchip contains identifying information that can be read by a scanner.

neuter (NOO-tuhr) to remove a male animal's reproductive glands.

nutrient (NOO-tree-uhnt) something found in food that living beings take in to live and grow.

pregnant having one or more babies growing within the body.

registry a place where official records are kept.

spay to remove a female animal's reproductive organs.

species (SPEE-sheez) living things that are very much alike.

vaccine (vak-SEEN) a shot given to prevent illness or disease.

ONLINE RESOURCES

To learn more about Bombay cats, visit **abdobooklinks.com**. These links are routinely monitored and updated to provide the most current information available.

INDEX